Words In Search of a Meaning

BY THE AUTHOR

Mormon Heroin

XXIII Epistles

Dun Scotus On His Sick Bed

Cartographies of Silence

Endings

Words In Search of a Meaning

Erik Vatne

BURNING
APPLE
PRESS

Published by Burning Apple Press
110 Chestnut Ridge Road
#166
Montvale, NJ 07645
Email: burningapplepress@hotmail.com

Typeset, front and back cover design: Liza Littlefield
    www.lizalittlefield.com
Back cover author photo: Self-Portrait, Rhinebeck, 1987
Courtesy of Author

Library of Congress Cataloging-Publication-Data

Vatne, Erik.
   Words in search of a meaning / Erik Vatne.
   p. cm.
   Poems
   ISBN: 13: 978-0615691985
   ISBN-10: 0615691986
   Library of Congress Control Number: 2012916449
Thanks: Penny Gibson for production services, Liza Littlefield for her design and help in realizing this project, Brendan, Gregg, Myrna, mother and the memory of Johnny Cash. I'd also like to acknowledge the team at CreateSpace for their professionalism.

Manufactured in the United States of America

For Dylan

"Something you cannot explain to another person is called 'nistar, "hidden," like the taste of food, which is impossible to describe to one who has never tasted it. You cannot express in words exactly what it is-it is hidden."

—Daniel C. Matt

"Words fail, there are times when even they fail…What is one to do then, until they come again."

—Samuel Beckett, *from*

'Happy Days'

"The real being, with no status, is always going in & out through the doors of your face."

—Lin-Chi

"I'm gonna get birth naked
And burn my old soul
And dance on its grave…"

—Bruce Springsteen

WORDS IN SEARCH OF A
MEANING

CONTENTS

BOOK I – WORDS IN SEARCH OF A MEANING

PART ONE

PART FOUR

ASKING AN INDULGENCE

all those years

offering poems as indulgences

against death; afraid

to accept what I already knew

in my heart-mind:

life is impermanent.

& so I wrote

obsessively & compulsively,

cuz poetry had saved my life.

& so I wrote my way into the poems

& every poem was an elegy,

every poem an epitaph.

so afraid to die,

using the very thing that saved me

as a shield against death.

I used words like shovels

digging my own grave.

I shouldn't be so hard on myself.

& now at this moment:

12:40am on May 24, 1994,

I bow & approach my desk

for what feels like the first time,

& set to put down with deep humility

the why that lead me to this place.

I am still frightened of the infinite white spaces

of the page,

the poem

& the life that resides in this little corner of my room

made sacred

by the sheer act of willing it into being.

I am still frightened of the urge towards the impossible

& offering the poems as indulgences

against death.

I am learning my way into language.

I am not afraid to say what I already know:

I am painfully aware that my small knowledge

Leaves me nowhere but here

WORDS IN SEARCH OF A MEANING

BOOK I

PART ONE

POEM AGAINST WORK

Open the window.

Let in the night air.

It is very cold.

Hear the rain?

Celebrate your insomnia!

Idiot,

Everything is an occasion for a poem!

To hell with work!

You were made for this moment.

1993

ALBA

even after

a night

of love

we awake

only to

inhale

dust mite

excrement

from satin

pillows

MATINS

I am interested in the way he is in the world

& his coming & going. The opening out

onto the precipice of available light.

The love rising at matins, filling

the blood from earlier sacrifice. The anointing

of each act of surrender with entirety of being.

He didn't have a choice. The actual change

that occurred was always alive inside him.

There was nothing but the waiting night.

REPORT

44° in Central Park

Light rain is falling

Monday April 15, 1996

11:00pm

PORTRAIT OF A MAN IN A ROOM

This is the place you always return.

The path leads you back to the source,

to the center of yourself. And whether you like it or

    not

the road returns to you and to that man in the room

staring helplessly into the darkness.

There is nothing but this:

this useless activity of arriving & departing,

of answering the silence

& attending to one's failure.

This is the place you always return.

This room.

This room that contains immensities.

GOING HOME

hell is a sleepless night

w/ the sky starting to

fill up w/ that sickly

blue liquid light & you're

driving home somehow

from NYC crossing the

GW w/ 1 hand over yr

eye after 24 hrs. of booze

& coke & cigarettes...&

the world is walking dead

as you gag on the stink

of exhaust from cars

warming up & they

too just want to be

left alone & the men

& women at sad bus stops

wait for their own private

hells to begin while you

are going home to Excedrin,

 the dry heaves & shakes

& Haydn on the radio

until you finally pass out

& if yr lucky won't puke

& choke on yr vomit &

call it *sleep* as the curtains

of love are closed against

the light of the world &

those nasty birds w/ their

paranoia & lies mocking

you w/ their ugly songs

& the smell of creosote

from the neighbor's driveway & then the lawn-

mowers & power tools

& smell of fresh cut grass

like yr first come when she

sucked you in the dugout

where you played baseball

as a child & snapped a

popper under yr nose

& you both called it *love*

…it was more than

that…it felt—for a

moment—like it was

the one moment—&

a door in yr life was

opened & you stepped

thru & were reborn into

innocence again…

not knowing that

all those years later

this is where you

would find yrself

dying to this light

RETURNING HOME

to return to a house

after a long exile I can't

call it a home it is not

my home it is a place

where I keep my stuff

I can't bring myself to

pretend otherwise the

other inhabitants retreat

to their rooms to whisper

& conspire it's not paranoia

just a fact the music is on

in the opposite room I turn

off the light & listen in

the dark Satie piano piece

I can't recall the title it's one

of my favorites it saves me

even for a moment because

I am suffering I am *losing*

it in this big house I am

claustrophobic & feel like

I am suffocating I want to

strip off my clothes & rush

out into the snow screaming

or weeping I want to go to

sleep in a cocoon of snow

where I can hear the soft

rustle of snow fall on the

three pines in the backyard

& never again have to hear

words like *divorce* & *failure*

I can't listen to those words

anymore I want a world

without their words I want

words filled with light & the

gentle tug at the heart of

things that make it all real

& worth living I am just a

man learning to speak a new

word I can't pronounce it

yet but I am trying to say it

to you but you are alone too

behind a locked door listening

to the piano music working out

your own exile until finally the

music stops & I leap up & open

my door I am so in love with my

sorrow Oh Lord I want the home of snow

RETURNING TO THE UNITED STATES AFTER A LONG EXILE

It's like going to the

Catskill Mts. for the

weekend & lying in a

wicker lawn chair &

inhaling the cool, sharp

aroma of the pines that

sway gently in the breeze

& all you can smell is

the hospital stink of

Pine-sol liquid disinfectant

or it's like listening to

the rolling stones play

Willie Dixon's little red rooster

EPITHALAMION

you go to your
  desk like a
furtive bride
on her wedding
  night & make
a poem with a
  #2 empire pen-
  cil or a bic
biro or a brother
  typewriter or a
Macintosh computer
  but you are
  not writing a
poem anymore than
  I am writing a
poem or proving
  a priori the ex-
  istence of God
or the ministry
  of angels

DABAR

The words

like eunuchs

in a harem

of images

1993

SOMEONE IS CALLING

something

calling out of the darkness

calls-

he answers

with no answer-

his poem

just answering

the other poem

1994

ALEXITHYMIA

for Ian Curtis

you answer

that which

precedes you

in darkness

in silence

you make

a poem

out of words

what else

do you have?

you could

settle

for less

1990

PART TWO

HOW TO MAKE A POEM NO. 1

1.) Make a poem with words.

2.) Make a poem without words.

3.) See what happens.

HOW TO MAKE A POEM NO. 2

1.) The first thing I did was make poems out of
     words.

2.) The second thing I did was make poems out
     of other things.

3.) That's when the trouble started.

1993

24 QUESTIONS

WHY THESE WORDS

WHY THESE WORDS INSTEAD OF OTHER

    WORDS

WHY THIS FORM

WHY THIS FORM INSTEAD OF ANOTHER

    FORM

WHY THESE WORDS

WHY THESE WORDS ARRANGED IN THIS

    PARTICULAR WAY

WHY THESE THOUGHTS

WHY THESE THOUGHTS INSTEAD OF OTHER

THOUGHTS

WHY THESE WORDS

WHY THESE WORDS INSTEAD OF OTHER

WORDS

WHY THESE THINGS

WHY THESE THINGS INSTEAD OF OTHER

THINGS

WHY THIS FORM

WHY THIS FORM INSTEAD OF ANOTHER

FORM

WHY THIS WORLD

WHY THIS WORLD ARRANGED IN THIS

    PARTICULAR WAY

WHY THIS WORLD INSTEAD OF ANOTHER

    WORLD

WHY THESE WORDS

WHY THESE WORDS INSTEAD OF OTHER

    WORDS

WHY THIS POEM

WHY THIS POEM INSTEAD OF ANOTHER

    POEM

WHY THESE WORDS

WHY THESE WORDS ARRANGED IN THIS

PARTICULAR WAY

WHY THESE WORDS

April 13, 1995
Paramus Park Mall
New Jersey

THIS / THAT

DID YOU WRITE THIS

DID YOU WRITE THAT

DID YOU SEE THIS

DID YOU SEE THAT

DID YOU SAY THIS

DID YOU SAY THAT

DID YOU THINK THIS

DID YOU THINK THAT

DID YOU READ THIS

DID YOU READ THAT

Gate Theatre
Dublin, Ireland
September 1991
for Samuel Beckett

SONNET

1.) Book

2.) Body

3.) Space

4.) Door

5.) Word

6.) Face

7.) Sigh

8.) Grain

9.) Root

10.) Shadow

11.) Man

12.) Body

13.) Book

14.) Light

BLACK MIRROR

for Roger Gilbert-Lecomte

junk	sick
spine	sutra
holy	resin

hot	sun
raw	meat
body	fluids

grace	period
grace	
tissue	saturation

black	bile
grace	

MAPS

This line is moving towards the right margin; hence,
the line is moving in a linear direction. As the line
moves to the right it creates its own narrative because
it is moving from Point A to Point B. Poetry is to be
found somewhere between those two points.
The It is a matter of physics.
The line is a prison of its horizontal movement. It
would like to remain
unbroken. It would like to keep moving off the page.
The poem does not want to be a prisoner caged
between two points. The line does not want to
submit to the tyranny of margins.
It considers its options.
Perhaps it could resist moving on a horizontal plane?
The line considers moving vertically.
There is gravity involved.
The poem contains depths and widths that cannot be
measured by any
instrument.
The line is restricted in its movement.
The poem is self-contained but ready to be released at
any moment.

1990

ATLAS

you are

like a

word with-

out mean-

ing. I am

trying

to de-

fine you.

this is

what we

do. we

compile

reports,

diagrams,

dictionaries,

charts,

atlases

of flesh.

do not

let me

do it.

you will

never

forgive

me.

DOOR

"The word 'door' is not the door, is it?"

— *Krishnamurti*

A door appears.

You open the door.

The door is open.

You open.

Out onto.

A space.

Landscape of.

You pause.

You fear.

It's there.

Waiting.

You wait.

You are there.

The door is.

Open.

You pass thru.

Or into.

Or out of.

What *is* falls away.

From you.

The door is a word.

It is dark.

It is out there.

It is in you.

It is light.

1996

GRID NO. 1

a line

breaks

here

& then

nothing

whether
i move

horizontal

or

vertical

i can

never

move

behind

the place

i

began

1994

POEM

the poem

begins w/

words-

sometimes

the poem

does not

begin w/

words.

the words

point to

places

that are

not poems-

sometimes

the poems

do not

contain

any words

LESIONS I

The pain brought you to language.

The language leads you to the pain.

You were lead to the words.

And you went in.

The pain leads you to poems.

The poems were offerings to that pain.

The language told you things about itself.

Lies lead you back to the truth of what was being said

    through that pain.

The language didn't absolve you.

You followed the poems into the pain.

The deepest part of it.

The part beyond language.

Beyond words like *pain*.

Writing into it.

The language betrayed you.

And you loved.

Beyond love.

And words like *love*.

You loved the poems.

You loved the language.

You loved the pain.

And the way into it.

There was no way out.

You were trapped.

In the living death of language.

And you remain there.

1995

LESIONS II

language yourself

language yourself into

language yourself into the pain

processed thru

processed thru the breath

thru the breath

language yourself

into the process

language yourself thru

language yourself thru the pain

thru the breath

process yourself

thru the pain

language yourself

thru the breath

into the silence

1995 - 1996

POEM WITH PEOPLE IN IT

Jennifer wants to know why there are no people in my
poems. I read somewhere once that if there are no people
in your dreams you could be crazy. There are always lots of
people in my dreams. Basically, my dreams are boring.
I never had a dream that a giant locust was laying eggs in
my mouth and I gave birth to a litter of hybrid
human/locust mutations.

I've often wondered why there are no people in my poems.
Does this mean that there might be something wrong with
me? I'll have to speak to my shrink, Dr. X about this. He's
quite eccentric but very cool. He loves art and digs Wallace
Stevens so that makes him an interesting guy in my book.
He sometimes falls asleep during our sessions. I am
probably telling him about one of my dreams. I like the
way he chews gum and takes it out of his mouth and roll it
back & forth on the couch in this repetitive motion. It
makes me think that things are going to be okay. That even
needed doctors and scientists are as crazy as the rest of us.

I don't know. I always felt uncomfortable mentioning
people in my poems. I don't have any problem talking or
dreaming about them but somehow poems are different.
I mean it looks weird to see names like Gertrude, Norman,
Cliff, Helen, Washington, Dylan, Jennifer, Tara, Jerry,
Steinar, Inger, Brendan, Aidan, Gregg, Joe, Mike, Christy,

Tony, Betty, Mary, Jackie. I have even probably forgotten some names. I would hate to leave anyone out. I guess a lot of people will be added or taken off this list someday.

I guess I just haven't been able to put any people in my poems. I don't want to be a namedropper, like a lot of poets. In many ways I am a blessed man. I love a lot of people but I'd never consider putting their names in a poem.

INCIDENTS

I attack a man in a wheelchair. I knock him off his chair and his limp body spills onto the carpet. I don't believe he is really crippled.

This Irish woman wants to marry me and have children. I am overcome with joy. We sneak off in the middle of the night and take a ferry to Cornwall. During the trip we meet an old man and he becomes our traveling companion. We go to a dance but I don't want to pay the admission price.

We are camping outside a hospital. A woman I've never met tells me she is pregnant. I faint. When I slowly fade back into consciousness I am told she had an abortion and died during the procedure. I realize I have been set up.

I am in a long, dark tunnel. I hear rats scurrying in the dark. I wade through the brackish water until I see an opening of light. Finally, I arrive at the opposite end of the tunnel. I look out into an old abandoned rock quarry. There are people in the quarry playing a game.

I am back at the dance. The chaperones are putting the chairs and tables away. Men and women are leaving together. There is much laughter and flirting to indicate their attraction to one another.

When I leave it is dark. The woman and old man are gone. I get on my bicycle and pedal quickly down a dirt road on the campus where I went to college.

Someone is chasing me.

SCENES FROM A LIFE

I'm in my study skimming through the *Norton Anthology of English Literature, Volume 1*. I am looking for something. I keep coming back to these anonymous songs like *Lord Randal* & *Westron Wynde*. I am trying to feel something. I am reminded of some form of magic and nostalgia that brought me here in the first place. I read a few of these early English lyrics and feel somewhat restored to sanity.

⋆

I put down the book and go turn on the radio. A song by Dionne Warwick, *If Anyone Had a Heart*, is playing. Suddenly I am back in Schraalenburg. I am nine years old. It's a warm summer night. I can't sleep because I know that there is something going on downstairs. I get out of bed quietly so as not to wake my younger brother. I tiptoe across the room into the hallway. I crouch down and pull my knees to my chest. I don't make a sound. I can see my mother downstairs on the couch looking out the window. She is smoking a cigarette. I am scared because I have never seen my mother smoke a cigarette.

*

My mother sits in the dark smoking and listening to
her Dionne Warwick records. She is playing the song,
If *Anyone Had a Heart* over & over. She is weeping
softly as she continues to look out the window. I am
filled with fear and sadness. I want to take away her
pain but I am frozen.

*

My father dropped her off after a party but must have
driven off somewhere where he can't be found.
What is it about this house and us that drives him
away?

*

My mother might be a little drunk herself. She weeps
and sings softly the words of the song. I sit on my
heels and stare into the dark room that's only lit by
the orange glow of the burning embers of her
cigarette. She doesn't know I am watching her but I
see and feel everything.

*

I am 14 years old. I come home stoned after doing
bong-hits all afternoon with my best friend. Our
family has an Irish terrier named Tara. I am too
stoned to talk to anyone so it's a good thing the
family is not home. I stand in the hallway staring at
our dog. I don't know what kind of a look it was but
it was one of those looks. Normally, she would be
barking and jumping up and down on me with joy
but she stares like she doesn't know me. I sway back
and forth grinning and she runs and hides under the
kitchen table. I am just standing there. I am not doing
anything to anyone.

*

I get up and turn off the radio. I go to my record
collection and pull out my Dionne Warwick records.
I sit in the dark smoking and listening to the music. I
am alone. My son is not sitting at the top of the stairs
watching me because he is living with his mother.

*

I can feel it all again, whatever it was. It has
something to do with being a kid growing up in the
New Jersey suburbs in the 1970's, wondering if my
father was going to come home alive.

*

We are all waiting for the phone to ring. We are
afraid of ringing telephones. We wait for the call from
the police or the hospital.

*

I am not drunk today.

1991

THE DAY FREDDY MERCURY DIED

Your family is driving to the Grand Opening of the Paramus Park Mall. They say it's going to be the biggest mall in New Jersey. They are all excited but you are filled with fear: the crowds, noise, and lights. You sit in the front seat because you get car sick and your mother and brother sit in the backseat of your father's brand new yellow Cadillac.

You have control of the radio. You find your favorite station: 102.7 WNEW. The DJ plays a newly released song called *'Bohemian Rhapsody'* by a group called Queen. You have never heard anything like this before; you turn up the radio. The rock and roll opera makes you feel alive and you disappear into the song. The last sad guitar notes play and the singer sings, *"Sometimes wish I'd never was born at all."* Your mother doesn't like those lines; they are so morbid, she says. But you understand. You don't feel alone; but now you feel painfully ashamed and self-conscious; as if some secret part of yourself has been exposed to your family. You feel the criticism of the song is a judgment on *your* feelings. You aren't comfortable listening to songs in their presence. You feel things so strongly and no one seems to understand. You cry and laugh sometimes for no apparent reason; but music has been your savior; since you were a little boy and hid the transistor radio under the covers at night and listened until you fell to sleep.

The next day you find out the song is from an album called *'A Night at the Opera.'* You know that's the title of your favorite Marx Brothers film. You take some of your allowance money and walk five miles along the railroad track to the next town to the nearest record shop; called *'The Camp.'* This is where all the stoners hang out. There is even a room in the back filled with black light posters and a fluorescent light where you can get high and sit and stare at the posters. There is one by the artist Robert Crumb of a man with a melting face. You buy the 45 single of *'Bohemian Rhapsody.'* You listen to the song over and over and the following week you buy the album. There is only one other boy in your class that knows the group and the song. You try and tell your friends about the band but they aren't listening to rock music; yet.

You cut a photo of Freddy Mercury out of *Creem* or *Circus* magazine. You start fantasizing about being a rock star. You have never seen a man with painted fingernails. You are drawn to the way he wields the mic stand in a sexually phallic and suggestive manner. You suddenly feel confused about your sexuality. You want to look like Mercury. You take the photo and walk around the corner to the old, Italian barber who cuts your hair. You take a number and when it's called you get up and walk to the chair and see yourself in the mirror.

"I want you to cut my hair like the guy in this photo," you say.

"Why would you wanna look like that" he asks? He looks like a fag." The men waiting to get their buzz cuts look up from their newspapers and cigarettes and laugh.

"He's not a fag," you say.

"I ain't never cut no hair look like this," he says. "Sit down and I'll see if I can turn you into a pansy-singer like this guy."

The men laugh again but don't look up from their papers.

You already have the longest hair of any boy in your class; surely the barber can make you look like the singer in the white satin jumpsuit.

You close your eyes.

"Well, what do you think, kid," he asks?

"It doesn't look like him," you say.

"Well, next time you wanna look like a girl go to the unisex salon uptown. Your hair is too long anyway."

You leave feeling shame and dejection. You look at the picture torn from the magazine and crumple it up and stuff it into your pocket.

You don't care what they say; you're going to be a rock star. You take guitar lessons and write your first lyric with a friend. You feel stupid and inept struggling through 'Go Tell it on the Mountain' at the guitar academy while you can hear a kid your age in the next room play the solo at the end of 'Stairway to Heaven' note for note. It's around this time you smoke your first joint on a warm, spring night under the elm trees in the wooded area overlooking the local golf course. You feel like you have arrived home in your body.

You abandon the guitar lesson and lyric writing to long afternoons getting high and listening to music. You continue to listen to Queen; but also Hendrix and especially Led Zeppelin. Suddenly, everyone is listening to Led Zeppelin and progressive -rock groups like Genesis and Yes and Pink Floyd, which are good for getting high. You begin to slowly lose interest in Queen after *'A Day at the Races'* is released; even though you listen to that album until it's worn down; but your new god is Jimmy Page.

One day you cut class and get high and sit around your friend's house and he asks if you jerk off.

"I'll show you," he says.

You are twelve years old.

The next year is spent getting high, listening to music and having sex with your friend and doing just enough work to graduate from 8th grade.

"I don't wanna be gay," he says.

You recoil.

"What do you mean *gay*," you ask? "Is that what this means? I don't understand. I'm not gay. I thought we were sharing love and affection. It's just sex."

He laughs.

"No. It means we're fags," he says. "I wanna date girls now. You better get yourself a girlfriend too before somebody catches us and thinks we're fags."

You turn your back to the wall and stare until the sunlight fills the room and get up and leave.

You never see him again.

*

In 1980 you meet your first wife. You are sixteen and she is fifteen. It's love at first sight. She is considered the most beautiful and desirable girl in town; but you are in love and going to be together forever.

She is going to perform in the talent show in high
school. She has choreographed a dance to the Queen
song 'Seaside Rendezvous.' You watch her practice
the dance steps many times. She paints and draws,
makes collages, and dances and sings. You know she
is going to be a big star someday. She reminds you of
Marilyn Monroe.

The night of the performance you stand at the back of
the theater and watch her dance on stage; your heart
bursting with love, admiration and joy. She is so
beautiful you want to weep. The performance goes
well.

When it's over she runs out the side door. You're
outside smoking a cigarette. She rushes into your
arms and begins to weep uncontrollably. She feels she
ruined the performance and everyone was laughing
at her. You hold her close and tight against your body
in the cold, October night. You light a cigarette and
put it to her lips. You reassure her the performance
went off without a hitch. "You were perfect. It was
beautiful," you say. You give her a single rose you
have been holding inside your leather jacket and the
two of you huddle together to keep warm. There is
no one else on the earth. She weeps and weeps into
your arms.

"It's going to be all right," you say. You say it and keep on saying it as it suddenly begins to snow and you fade into your own private sorrows. "I love you" you say. You keep saying and saying it over and over again in the desperate hope that someday she will believe.

November 24, 1991
Dublin, Ireland

ETUDE (FIVE FINGER EXERCISE)

Listening to Chopin although it's not really Chopin
playing him being dead and all it's this other guy I
forget his name but I don't mean I am listening to this
guy play he's not here in this room or anything like
that it's actually a record of this guy playing Chopin I
mean playing his I mean Chopin's piano music not
playing Chopin like he's an instrument because that
would be ridiculous and him long dead and all
although I guess the bones could be arranged and
played but not like a piano which is the plucking of
strings or rather striking of strings this would have to
be striking of bones to make a sound and it wouldn't
sound anything like this of course but he's not playing
Chopin his music of course at this moment either but
you never know he could be playing Chopin at this
very moment although it's kind of late here on the
East Coast but if he was in California he could be
playing it's earlier there although I just can't picture
anyone playing or listening to Chopin in California I
mean when I think of Chopin I think of Dublin or
Copenhagen not even Paris or Poland for some
reason I'm not sure why that is well perhaps even
Prague yes I would go so far as to say Prague but he
wouldn't be playing Chopin in those cities because
it's too late or too early to be playing Chopin in those

cities even though at some time and place he played
this piano music of Chopin and it was recorded on
this record I mean CD for some reason I still keep
calling them records or albums all I know is that at
this very moment maybe somewhere in a small room
this guy is listening to some other guy play Chopin I
mean you never know about these things it's a sad
beautiful world full of crazy coincidences

1992

NO THANKS, JUST LOOKING

The rain falls and I want to compare it to something
else or rely on the old Western metaphysics of binary
opposites but if I say the rain falls like this or that I am
also saying it's not like something else therefore
negating the empirical experience of the rain actually
falling but old habits die hard and I hate dead
metaphors but they are part of the dramatic
hyperbolic speech I inherited from my mother and
the vernacular of my tribe I would still like to weave
a metaphor into this playing because I still believe the
metaphoric impulse is at the heart of the poetic
impulse but I have always been contrary and perverse
as mother said so I made a conscious decision to
abandon such accoutrements of the trade and maybe
it's just a little too didactic for me even though that's
probably not what I meant to say but I have always
rejected the didactic in literature and totally disagree
with Shaw who said something to the effect that all
literature is didactic I should look that word up again
I was once called auto-didactic and took it as an
insult but it's true I was and am and I think all poets
despite their levels of education or mis-education or
how many letters follow their names on business
cards or letter head are still primarily autodidactic but
I don't think it's primarily true because poems can be

like these totally autonomous and organic structures
that merely refer to their own making and that is why
I like poems that are about nothing although I think
some philosopher somewhere once made the
assertion or put forth the theory or is it a proposition
well whatever you call it that to presuppose *a priori* a
nothing suggests something I don't recall who wrote
that perhaps it was Parmenides but I'm not really sure
since I don't know much about philosophy and I'm
certainly not an academic or intellectual it's just a
hobby of mine to think like this sometimes when I
get bored it's even kind of a goof but it wasn't to my
wife no sir she hated philosophy and when I would
drop words like Existentialism or names like
Nietzsche she'd just cringe and sometimes get really
pissed off and scream at me about other things like
laundry and changing the baby's diaper and such I
mean she would really act put out and in pain if I
tried to engage her in a stimulating conversation but I
think looking back on it that she was afraid of
philosophy because she wasn't much for thinking or
reflecting too deeply on things and as a matter of fact
the more I think about it the more I realize she was
just plain scared and stuff but maybe I'm mistaken in
assuming such things myself because like I said I'm
certainly not the brightest bulb in the bunch either it's
only that I like to think about stuff occasionally like
this night with the rain falling and my wife long gone
and looking out the window I wanted to say

something about the rain falling and compare it to
something else because that's what poets do and
maybe I'll never be a poet either because when I look
out at the falling rain all I see is the falling rain and it
is beautiful and fills my heart with such a feeling I
would like it to be raining and to hear it on the
rooftop on my last day on this beloved earth but I
guess that means I won't be writing anything else
about the rain I think I have said enough already and
besides it's late and there are better things to do than
sit around philosophizing

September 4, 1991

POEM

for Dylan

Ouch, it hurts
he says

as I wrap
a Band

Aid around
his finger:

This is
not a

poem:
we just

like the
sound of

the word
ouch

BLUE

for Derek Jarman

The simple fact

of your lust

made visible

on the bed

the blue screen

a Pascalian

diversion from

your impending

death as the body

lets go into it

and returns

to the source

LIVES OF THE SAINTS

when I say myself inside you

I am speaking for everybody-

including all the Gods and Saints

even the ones you've never heard of

1993

FEVER

the bliss

of the dream

last night

watching

the actress

Nastassja Kinski

doing cartwheels

in the sunlight

while you painted–

and the sadness

of this day

nothing but

bronchitis

and poetry

CAMEO

why can't

you say

something,

anything,

she says,

something.

anything.

1993-1994

YOU ONLY LIVE ONCE

she said,

we don't

even

live once.

LIVES OF THE ARTISTS

she fills

a page

w/ poems

& draw-

ings &

asks me

what I

think of

her work–

a man

will always

lie to

a naked

woman

reclining

on a

futon

in Boston

1993

SPLEEN

after we made love

(which is just a polite

term for fucking) she

wanted to smoke &

talk & watch Dave

Letterman on TV (&

that was the worst part

of it) I just wanted to

lie in bed & listen to

the house settle with

the weight of my sadness

1992

HEAVEN

sometimes when I am watching

the television, particularly shows

like *The Mary Tyler Moore Show*

or *Bugs Bunny* or *The Honeymooners*,

or even the movie *Hercules in*

America, which was Arnold

Schwarzenegger's first movie;

(although they dubbed his voice

on account of the thick Austrian

accent), at 4am on Saturday

October 30, 1992 on channel 7,

I suddenly realize that there is no

such thing as death or suffering

& I know that I am going to live

forever in that TV paradise that

religious folks refer to as Heaven

SOUNDTRACK TO A LIFE NOT LIVED

way back in the mix

the muddy sounds of lovers

muted by drums

1983

STILL LIFE WITH CUM SHOT

translated from the Japanese of Hiro Hosokawa

The sperm on your face

is just a footnote

to the actual ontological mystery

you find yourself facing

at this moment

WHAT SHE SAID TO HIM

do you

see what

I'm saying,

she says?

he sees

her words

like cones

or spirals

spinning

out of her

body

but says

nothing

YOU HAVE A WAY WITH WORDS

he says

he envies

her way

with words:

she speaks

and writes

as if

they have

meaning

1995

POEM 4

she says

she reads

between

the lines

of my

love poem

some words

I didn't

write but

were written

by her

for me

to read

1993

POEM 5

you are

not like some-

thing else-

you are

like no-

thing else

not even

this poem

1994

WIFE

for I.K.

So far I've spoken a lot about my wife

But I haven't said anything

Wife is just a word

I've used lots of words

I talk about my wife

But where is she?

I see the word *wife*

I've walked up and down

And to and fro

In this poem

And I still can't find

My wife

Only the word *wife*

And I don't know

What that word means anymore

Wife

A thin slice of a word

Like a willow reed

A sigh of a word

Vowels and consonants

Married to one another

In perfect union

In that at one syllable

Joined together

Let no man tear asunder

This word mocks me

Defies me to define it

Wife smirks in the knowing

I can't

I don't know what it means

What any of it means

And that is why I keep saying it

Over and over

Like a sacred mantra

But my wife knew she was just a word

After all those years

She became a word

She was part of my secret room of words

And that is why she left me

Or why I like to think she left me

Whether it is true or not

It doesn't matter

When she left

She took the words with her

So no matter how many times

I say the word *wife*

Or write the word *wife*

She'll never be here

In this poem

1990

SPELL AGAINST HIS WIFE'S LOVER

You're going

to make

a poem

& break

into their

house &

hide it

under

the bed

where they

sleep &

make love

& when

he gets

out of

bed the

next day

to put

on his

shoes for

work he'll

see the

folded up

piece of

paper &

he'll pick

it up

& read

it &

die

1991

CONSPIRACY AGAINST DREAMING

they don't

know what

to say

about

the poem

even

the ones

who think

they know

what to

say don't

know what

to say

instead

they say

something

anything

what they

say isn't

the poem

1994

MUSICA UNIVERSALIS

the noise

a poem makes

in his mind:

unlike anything

you've heard

or imagined

READING BONES

for Brendan

you go to the bookcase

& select a book from

the rows of books neat-

ly arranged on shelves

where the dust of a

thousand years has

settled with spoors,

dust mite excrement

& strokes of your long

brown hair that have

fallen upon the spines-

it is a hardcover book-

the book has lots of words

between the covers-you

bring the book back to bed

& pull up the covers &

settle in as the rain falls

on the rooftop & you

browse lazily through the

book staring inertly at

the words in the book-

you are looking for some-

thing to affirm or deny

it doesn't matter anymore

as long as it points the way

to that other world waiting

for you beyond the room

& the bed & the cracks

in the ceiling & the boot

scuffed wooden floors-

you reach into the book

& move into the empty

spaces of the book as the

covers of the book close

behind you shutting out

the white noise & light-

you have been doing this

your whole life or at least

for the past 14 years & you

wonder when will you stop

doing the same thing over

& over again & expecting

different results?

LUCKY STRIKES

smoke outside my window

who the hell is smoking

& stalking in the backyard

another American serial

killer on the loose crushing

my flowers while I recline

in the dark room, alone,

rudderless, bereft, withdraw-

ing from heroin, alcohol,

nicotine & love what's worse

listening to the katydids make

their awful music in the trees

& / or staring into an empty

bookcase at a broken lava lamp

circa 1976 missing & loving all

the wives, lovers & children

of the world & wanting to smoke

so bad I should fill up my lungs

with the breath of god instead

or at least a lover her mouth on

mine inhaling & exhaling the

sweet erotic perfume of her

whore's breath oh it doesn't matter

my breathing has been shallow

& wheezy & anxiety ridden now

for years & I am not stupid

I know this is nothing more

than another sacred diversion

from the real pain I know

Saint Pascal was right so I pray

POEM 6

she says

he goes

so far

& deep

into

the poems

he forgets

how to

live

& love

outside

the core

of silence

1996

TRANSLATIONS

all the poems he writes

are like translations

from the dead

DETOURS

you tried

to write

about

something

but you

couldn't-

as soon

as you

started

to write

about

something,

something

else would

start writing

about

itself-

so you

abandoned

the act

of writing

about

anything-

something

else always

got in the way.

FOR DYLAN

my son,

you are

not *my*

son. you

are not

even

our son.

you *are.*

TWO FIGURES IN A LANDSCAPE

for Dylan

My son asks me what this word means. I answer him
with more words. I know

I haven't answered him. I am just talking about
language.

My son asks me what this thing is. I answer him with
still more words. I

haven't answered him.

How can I tell him what this thing means. He
already knows it more intimately

than I ever will. I haven't told him what this thing is.
I don't know what this

thing is.

We are both new to this. We are both new to this
language. We are new to the things of this life.

I only think I know what this word means. I am just
talking about language.

We are so alone together.

We are playing in the park. There is something over there that others have

called trees. I see something resembling a sky.

My son asks me what a poem means.

I answer him with more words. I haven't said anything about the poem. I am

talking about language. I am trying to get there.

I cannot name that which cannot be named. I cannot speak of such things.

We are so alone together.

My son digs in the sand. My love for him has no words. When I say this I am

painfully aware that I have said too much and not enough.

We are talking about language.

We are so alone together.

1992

WHAT WE THINK WE MEAN

We make a poem

& say,

"This

is the world."

But it isn't.

The poem

is always

about some-

thing else,

even if

it says

it is about

this or that.

Language

took the world

apart,

but it can't

put it back

together.

PART THREE

MT. TREMPER

time was

I wrote down

everything

couldn't contain

or wait too

had to

and did

and now

nothing

but gray robes

silences

rain

without end

POEM 7

no poem

outside

my self

no poem

outside

language

no poem

inside

my self

no poem

inside

language

no poem

above

my self

no poem

above

language

no poem

beyond

my self

no poem

beyond

language

no poem

beneath

my self

no poem

beneath

language

no poem

around

my self

no poem

around

language

no poem

inside

my self

no poem

outside

language

no poem

within

my self

no poem

within

language

no poem

without

my self

no poem

without

language

no poem

inside

the poem

no poem

inside

language

no poem

outside

the poem

no poem

outside

language

no poem

without

my self

no poem

without

the poem

no poem

within

the poem

no poem

within

my self

WHERE YOU LIVED

there is

the place

and there

is the

word.

you had

been to

both.

the word

is where

you lived.

GRID NO. 2

what is

true & real

is what is

in the middle

of the beginning

& ending

of all meaning

WAITING

he can't

wait until

it's over

& he

can get

back home

& talk

about it

until it

is real

EXILE

a tree

stands

in the

desert:

it does

not stand

in the

desert

1992
Dublin

POEM WITHOUT WORDS

for Tom Segrich

you say

you are

not good

at putting

words in-

to words-

you have

trouble

finding

the word

for the

word. we

know what

you mean.

we can't

find the

word for

the word

either-

so we

made this

poem with-

out words

for you

instead.

1993

SAYING THINGS

for Genie

you say things

you say words

the words are things you say

the things you say are words

words are the things you say

say words

say things

say words and things

square words

round words

rectangular words

Genie's words

Genie's bunny walk

square words in round holes

round words in square holes

recode your world

with verbal labels

where words fail

you find yourself again

in the ether

observing the austerities

shaking out the poison

transubstantiations

tenebrous

toward the thorax

aposiopesis

do you see

do you see what I'm saying

do you hear

do you hear what I'm saying

1996

UNTITLED

this poem

has its own origin

its own way of entering

the empty space

and taking up temporary residence

in the ether

it attempts something

unknowable

it leaves the ashes

of its absence

on my tongue

LABYRINTH

he enters

he enters a space

the space he calls home

where only language can heal

he wants to enter a place

that even language cannot reach

he hides in the absences

God withdraws into shadow

1993

NO POEM

for the

poems

he saves that

part of him–

self no

one knows

about –not

even the poems

THE OFFAL

whose language

grunts or screams

out of my body

out of the trauma

my body searches

for a form

& finds (only

the inherited

silent net

it digs

thru the offal

to get to

God's viscera

the pre-language

state of

Being

he feels

& knows

in body-house

of poem

to protect

the tightening

& spasms

in sphincter

as it releases

& let's go

of its hold

on language

even if

his body

rebels

against the

form

of language

imposed on him

by the others

this *I*

originates

out of

nothing

but

the flesh-house

of words

& in the body

he finds

a form

for the impossible

afterword

1993

DUN LAOGHAIRE PIER, 1991

for Janet

"Loose your mind and come to your senses."

—*Fitz Perls*

I didn't bring my *pain* to the last session.

I mean I didn't bring my pain to the last poem.

I told you things.

I told how I walked to the end of Dun Laoghaire pier

in the dark:

I thought I would find God.

I watched the Sealink Ferry sitting still in the harbor.

I watched the yellow lights of Dublin in the distance.

I heard voices echoing across the bay.

Perhaps these were the voices of the men and women

That would break into my flat each night

I stand and outside my bedroom door, talking and

laughing.

153

As I tried to tie a knot for the rope

I bought at Costello's hardware store

On Patrick Street

While I wept and shook from DT's.

I don't think that was God speaking to me.

I told you I had spoken to my wife on the phone,

How she told me she needed me to sign the papers

Because she was going to marry someone else after

     the divorce.

I told you these things.

But I didn't bring my *poem* to the session;

I mean pain.

February 27, 1992

LAST DAYS

a sliver of ice on dry lips

1996

THE LOVERS

"There is no room," he said.

But there was room.

There is always room.

1996

PART FOUR

WHY I DON'T LOOK BACK

each poem

is a door

I have already passed thru-

when I look back

I see a pillar of salt

crumbling in the wind

August 25, 1996
Woodstock, New York

THRUST

living flecks of mica

flashing

in the *illuminati* of rain-

and beyond that

a wood thrush sings

from the burning throat

of a dead god

1996

EXILE IN ALEXANDRIA

a voice

but whose?

I like my loneliness,

sadness;

alone

with Cavafy

& Bach.

nothing

I have to do

but breathe

in

& breathe

out

COMING INTO TOUCH

for Norman O. Brown

you tried

to enter

that place

inside your-

self where

there are

no words-

only a place

of fear

& shame

residing

in the belly-

centered

in your sex,

paralyzing

you, nearly,

& she took

you into that

dark place

somehow-

you were blind-

folded, bound

& gagged-

but you still

tried to name

that feeling-

the feeling

without words

or images-

but without

the words

you were frightened

& felt

like a child

wanting to be held

& rocked

back & forth,

brought

into touch

& saved

by the tender

mercy of her

healing hands-

so you let go

& opened

out into

the lightness,

& stood

in the doorway

looking

for the first time

TEST RESULTS

the bio-chemical

poem event

without implosion

transmitter

the immune system

listening

cellular memory

of poem regression species

inertia

these libidinal investments

the poem

unit of energy

part of the post-human

apocalypse

no transmutation necessary

cells

gut feeling

and negates itself too

1995

WHAT HAPPENED

No matter how prepared you are

Or how prepared you think you are

You will never be prepared for this

And this is *now*

And beyond that there is nothing

1996

SAMSARA

countless

lives / deaths

already

inside me.

words

to words.

nothing

outside

of them.

1996

ELEGY

"The map is not the territory."

—Alfred Korzybski

in the end

you found the names

words

not the things:

    1.)   represented
    2.)   stood for
    3.)   signified
    4.)   symbolized

you lived

in a verbal world

not an extensional world

you carried this false map

of the world

in your head

1992-1993
Denmark, Norway, Ireland

AGAINST THE VISUAL

visual interference

indicates bodies

moving closer to

the embroidered

geometric designs

loose threads

scopic patterns

it all breaks up

it is pornography

it is what you are

1992

THE SECRET ART OF POETRY

This poem is like the man dressing up in his wife's
lingerie. The poem is parading around the bedroom
in its black bra, panties, garters and high heels. The
face is a mask of garish nightmare: blue eyeliner,
long fake lashes, bight ruby red lipstick, red rouged
cheeks and blonde wig. This poem is a great secret,
hidden from sight. The poem dances around the
room admiring itself in the full-length mirror. The
poem catches itself falling in love with its own
extinction. It sings and dances and even has moments
of ecstasy, like St. Theresa. This poem is beyond its
own understanding. It is not even subtle. The wife is
at work. The children are at school learning to read
and write. They are studying the secret art of poetry.

1991

TIRED

just

so

tired

of talk-

ing

about

my-

self to

priests

doctors

healers

teachers

therapists

so tired

of taking

these words

into my mouth

so tired

of explaining

my-self

to you

I'm so tired

of talking about

my-

Self

in these poems

1994

IN PRAISE OF A GOOD LIFE

for Max Jacob

why complain, *mon frère,*

when you can stay up all night

listening to the rain fall on the roof

while John McCormack singS Bach's,

Jesu, Joy of Man's Desiring

over & over again?

you are sober & alive.

you make poems out of words,

& even if she doesn't read them

it don't mean a thing.

in the morning

the sky will lighten in Paris

& Persephone shall rise again from the Dreamworld

& feed you the pomegranate of sleep

PORTRAIT OF GIRLS ON A BUS IN DUBLIN

These girls with their green skirts, black shoes, white
stockings, white blouses,
blue sweaters and red and white striped ties.
These girls with their hair tied back in ponytails.
These girls jumping on and off buses.
These girls that whisper secrets to each other.
These girls that giggle in small groups.
These girls that blush and avert their eyes.
These girls that sneak their first cigarettes but don't
inhale.
These girls that cluster in groups and carry satchels
filled with books and secret
notes.
These girls that are going somewhere nice.
These daughters.
These girls that have no sins to confess.
These girls that are going to live forever.

November 13, 1991
Monkstown,
Co. Dublin, Ireland
46A Bus

POEM BEGINNING WITH A LINE BY BATAILLE
AND ENDING WITH A LINE BY DESNOS

That one great poem was being elaborated

So that all words would fail further on

1995

LAST RITES

there's nothing

left to say

but the words

keep coming-

they are

so useless

& beautiful

I could

almost

love them

again

ASKING A BLESSING

When I am an old man

There will be no more need of reading

I will give all my books away

I will carry a lifetime of words in my head

And say them over to myself until the wolves arrive

There will be no more need of talking

My throat will be ravaged by the weight of the words

I spoke into the world

There will be no more need of writing

I would have disappeared into the texts

I will give myself over to a bowl of soup

As if this single act was some kind of benediction

1991

SOMATIC REVELATION

Opening of the sacrum = somatic revelation

taking place.   Energies & spaces inside the body are

being rearranged to the radical change in modalities.

God is like a virus invading his body.   The Christ

within him.   He is converted to the silence.   There

are myriad textual possibilities.   Probabilities.

Impossibilities.   What is available occurs anyway.

No control.   A night devoted to this magic.

1993

STORY

This is the only story worth telling. I mean
everyone's got a story to tell and they're all equally
important, but this is the only story worth telling for
me on a personal level. I guess I've been trying to tell
this story for the longest time, as long as I've lived it,
but I wasn't able or capable of telling it until now.

I'll tell you why it took so long. It had something to
do with running away from the story, trying to
escape from it and all that; out of fear I guess, but I
realize now that that's the only story that ever really
mattered to me.

This is going to be a story but I am not making any of
it up. It's all true. I mean it really happened. And I
am not going to change the names to protect the
innocent because we're all guilty.

I think I am just about ready. I'm going to tell the
story now.

November 10, 1991
Belfield,
Co. Dublin
Ireland

OPENING THE BOOK

When you wake up one day & realize that their language is a system of lies you will feel lost, frightened & alone. You will also be strangely & inexplicably liberated.

Finally, you will be free from your beliefs. You will no longer cling to your ideas or projections. You will not know where to turn. You will not know how to believe in anything anymore.

You will be at the place of dead words.

Your body is like a book.

Your body is a book.

The book has been opened.

THE FLESH HOUSE

for Marcel Marceau

What the movement means

And the tenderness of that living body

As it was born and made love and died

Without moving

The suchness of our condition

Is almost too much to say

That we have these bodies

That houses this absolute and impossible love

I feel for you

As you sleep upstairs

In this Victorian house

In San Francisco

This is what makes me weep

The meaning

I was searching for all these years

Revealed

In the movement

And it was something, my love,

Approaching grace

Tuesday October 19, 1999

Chateau Tivoli

ADHESIONS

BOOK II

desert ennui
realizable world
change, revise
laws of failure
and poetry

---

voice

(s)

ransom

threads

as

love

night's

       alembic

  recall

     on

   his

  lips

fibers of
alembic recall
cancel lesions

visions

desecrate

the

restless

veins

of

death

this

language

moment

embodies

tongues

outside

the

texts

opening

outside

the

texts

the

tongues

opening

outside

the

texts

falsify

    language

        shorn

           saturnalia

---

voice /

over

(narrative)

interrogation

AXIOM

---

root of this language charm
empty bellies
chaos the intervened dryad

sutures

of

endorphin

oppressed

love

genital aphasia abandons fences

smell

of

fear

sex

on

noetic

platitudes

east

lattice work

of frozen birds

squinting

through the rain

scrolls

of intestines

on the precipice

rain

on the trellis

of her thigh

---

turn

new

sky

around

hair

her

around

new

hair

fan

to

make

face

brush

bones

spasms

trespass

against

closets

of

absolved

liturgical

lust

---

noise/eyes   sentinel/lumbus   gods/lion

agony

Uni   /

form

less

apprehension

home

of

text   /

ward

thighs

signal

---

tissue

saturation

music

on the wing

spine

ecstasy

---

vitrines
in blue light

open

---

mandala

thighs

nothing

original

neowe

---

no   congenital   lies   speech

body

    always

       returns

           always

             alone

               always

                   here

mean

less

on

bed

omni

ABOVE

mourn/

(ing)

my S E L F

(ego)

in

relation

to

what

(is)

(was)

ABSENCE
is
LOCUS
of
(con)
TEXT

fabric of amputated landscapes
taciturn
sunken basement
luminous sin

infusing

(her)

severe

tissue

(with)

meaning

nothing

escapes

semblance

———————

penance

nomad

sans

system

such

music

splinters

UNINTERRUPTED

the non-linear
arrangement of viscera
leaves the tran-
sub-
stantiation
partially obscured
by the umbilicus
of reason

embryonic bridges transform function w/ becoming

in/

script

(ion)

ic

locus

X

o nomad

use me

sing me

yr system

of goat sacrifice

eidolon

talisman

---

sticky

secretions

of shadows

and ash

archives

rain

voices

follicles

Viscera lead nowhere

Ash

as

/ is

remains

SO

2 speak

elusive

syringe

(UN)

finish

(ed)

for

l
imago
s
s

In/

sects

(k)

not

(s)

end

THE OPENING OF THE HEART

BOOK III

for Bill Viola

Where does one stand

to allow
the experience

to enter
oneself

and what
the dark tells of us

as we set up camp

looking for a good spot
to rest

Orange glow of the red

what is a sky
that says so little

of who we are

there is something
in that hole

why we wait
is the answer
to its mystery

the boat
is not a ship

it is a vessel of course

where is it going
across

the water
doesn't know
it's coming

bystanders
are passengers

waiting
for departure

we go
from us

has it happened

is it going to happen

when they leave
have they left

anything

a typical day

voices

birds

crickets

water flooding
a house

street

if it doesn't
suggest
anything

don't worry

it will

eventually

they are spreading out now

the people
in the room

when they hear
the motor
start up

it is not the only thing
that moves them

an American siren sound

you know
that thing
about fire

how
it is always
there

going about

that means something

if you look inside
the saying

walking
back and forth

across

the white façade

looks like *stucco*

one likes how that sounds
before
the water starts

I could have told you that

the crowd
is thinning out

even the other ones

heavy
with their leaving

stuck

vertically in the frame

meet me later
would you

I'll be downstairs
by the fountain

looking up

spirals
like turds
seashells

for Nam June Paik

a garden
of television sets

tuned on
or
turned on
to
oh something

---

a procession

nobody is wearing a uniform

we've got to help each other
to get there

a hand
on a shoulder

but even so

still

a roaring sound
as the deluge

starts

it catches up with some of us

chapel

panel

chapel

panel

chapel

panel

I crouched down today

not often do I do that

but I did

and after awhile

my knees hurt

and I had to get up

and walk around

walk it off

didn't want

pins and needles

numb feeling

in legs

the rain
stopped

and then
started up
again

the sky
didn't change

how that was

remained
the same

its hues

variations

not withstanding
in my perception
of it

we finally
had to call it off
and go home

we left behind
nothing
but our leaving

renewal

going

taking things with you

waiting

vespers in the vestibule

dying apparatus

rose on bedside table

hand touches his forehead

she wipes a tear away while
the others

set out

towards what is between
those mountains

in the doorway

you will find
what you are looking for

abandon

how you have
to let it

happen to you

you will see
what I mean

and what that means
when she comes

down

the stairs

and turns to the left
and walks away
from what the others

doubt

at first

at first
I thought it was fire

but on closer inspection
I realized
it wasn't

warm fluid

like I wanted womb to be
when I was starting out
for the first time
at fifteen

swimming in it

all red and orange

and the doorway

a frame of light

and figures

disappearing

into the white spaces

while all around them
amniotic dreams

I've got to be present
when it happens

I've waited this long
with the rest of them

I am still patient
and devout

between

moving
and dying

the going part

all the same

as it does
and the music
increases

the tension
of strings

locks turning in doors

lights turned off

somehow
it all ended

abruptly

and got back to

as if
it had never happened

but changed me

as I go on

NOTES

Words in Search of a Meaning consists of all the work, excluding my book-length poem, *Cartographies of Silence* (Station Hill Press, 2009) written from 1990-1996 that I choose to preserve. The poems were mostly written in Ireland and New Jersey; as well as Norway and Denmark. I am happy to have them collected here as almost every poem I write is written in service to a unified collection that tells a story; even if the poems appear as fragments.

I am reminded of Agnes Martin's refusal to be labeled a *'minimalist;'* but rather an 'abstract expressionist.' I certainly understood what some poet-friends meant when they said they were "too minimalist" or asked for "more." (Two of the most *overused* critical clichés in the American poetry workshop lexicon are *"more"* or *"less."*) But these poems—if they are poems or not don't concern me—were my attempts to sustain a *dream- sequence* that I felt was under spiritual attack; and was due to my own spiritual odyssey to save myself and the 'dream' from being destroyed. I am happy to say that I am a blessed man and that *writing through* this process is why I am still writing today.

I didn't 'plan' to write in these *styles* or *forms*—my only aesthetic principle was to *"be naked"* and try and escape from my academic background, which I felt did more harm to me as a poet; but it arose out of necessity more than choice. At the time I had no templates or models for these pieces so chose not to publish any of the poems. I am grateful my "guardian angel" had me wait twenty years for this collection to come to be in the world. However, I have been amused to observe the coming and going of trends in the American poetry 'scenes' in the last twenty years. I referred to these pieces as my *vertical poems* and hoped they would be a bridge to a new world, life and poetry. I've been lucky; but also kept writing—and like Winston Churchill said: *"If you're going through Hell; keep going."*

What is more interesting—to me—is how this manuscript survived. I must have known there were a trilogy of books here because in 1999 I retyped the manuscripts—titled them—and completed the trilogy after seeing the Bill Viola video installation. Even though the final section was composed in 2002 it was very much in the style of writing I was doing in the mid- 1990's with *Cartographies* and knew it would be the closing—and opening—of the trilogy.

However, in 2005, I lost the manuscript. I had no other copy and the original copies of the poems had long been lost or destroyed. As a student of Carl Jung I was struck by the synchronicity that occurred when I *accidently* discovered the complete manuscript in an old suitcase only a week or two after publishing the massive 400+ page collection *Mormon Heroin* this year.

I certainly didn't want to take on another project of revising, editing and assembling a large manuscript until I realized this was the final exorcism that would allow me to let go and release another part of my past that preceded *Mormon Heroin*. I am grateful for the small blessing to publish these poems and release these old ghosts from the suitcase. I am relieved that this journey is complete. I welcome the reader with humility and gratitude. Thank you for taking this journey with me.

Book I: *Words in Search of a Meaning*: I feel a quick note here is necessary to explain *why* this book consists of so many poems 'about' poems. I am not sure I would have continued writing 'poetry' if I hadn't been able to write myself out of this trap: what happens when you wake up one day and suddenly don't know *how* to write a poem? If I was going to survive as a poet I felt I had no choice but to write what I could about *what* a poem *was* and was NOT; and this dark period lasted about four years. In this book I described what I was doing as a *forensics linguist*. I needed to write the confessional pieces as well as the *no-poems*; and in *Book II: Adhesions* to take the *poem* apart to see what was inside it before I could put *it*—and myself—back together again.

DABAR is transliteration from Hebrew character for 'word'. I should mention that my transliteration has been disputed by some friends that know Hebrew. I deferred to the original source taken from Fran Ferder's book *Words Made Flesh: Scripture, Psychology & Human Communication,* Copyright 1986 by Ave Maria Press; which I read in Dublin in 1991-1992. This book was so important in my spiritual journey that it remains in my night-table bookcase.

24 QUESTIONS was part of the Business Card Poem series I began at the Paramus Park Mall in 1995 and referenced in my book *Mormon Heroin.*

THIS/THAT: I cut class to attend a Beckett play that afternoon. I arrived in Dublin to attend graduate school at UCD in the summer of 1991. In August I was staying at a B&B in Sandycove and struck down with a severe case of influenza. I was so fatigued I was bedridden for two weeks. I had the good fortune of staying with a kind, older couple that took care of me and treated me like a family member; bringing me meals, liquids and medicine while I recuperated. I lay in that bed in the old Georgian room with the high ceiling and read every Beckett play—I had only read *Godot* and *Krapp's Last Tape* prior to this experience—and the trilogy of novels. I left that room a different man.

ATLAS: This poem was written for a drunken woman at the Kingston Bar who asked me to write her a "love" poem. I don't know how the poem survived. My buddy and I said we would be back in an hour. Four hours later I collapsed on Leeson Street after the almost fatal OD and spent the next two days in the hospital. I survived; along with the poem. I never saw the woman again.

STILL LIFE WITH CUM SHOT is a translation of a poem by the Japanese poet Hiro Hosokawa, born in 1987. My Japanese friend Daido is friends with his mother. He gave him copies of my books and a few weeks later I received an email from Hiro telling me about his life as a *Hikikomori* as well as a collection of poems called *Bukkake*. He spends his days and nights playing video games, writing poetry, reading and playing guitar. I don't know Japanese but he asked if I would consider translating his book. I don't have the time to work on such a project but with the help of a Japanese dictionary and exchange of emails managed a few different translations of this poem.

STILL LIFE WITH CUM SHOT

The sperm on your face
is just a footnote
to the actual historical dilemma
you find yourself facing
at this moment

STILL LIFE WITH CUM SHOT

The semen on your face
is just a footnote
to the actual historic dilemma
you find yourself facing
at this moment

STILL LIFE WITH CUM SHOT

The cum on your face
is just a footnote
to the historical dilemma
you find yourself facing
in this moment

STILL LIFE WITH CUM SHOT

The sperm on your face
is just a footnote
to the actual historic crisis
you find yourself facing
at this moment

STILL LIFE WITH CUM SHOT

The sperm on your face
Is just a footnote
To the ontological crisis
You find yourself facing
In this moment

STILL LIFE WITH CUM SHOT

The sperm on your face
Is just a footnote
To the ontological mystery
You find yourself facing
At this moment

THE SECRET ART OF POETRY is the earliest surviving poem from my unpublished collection *Man Imitating a Cloud*, which contains poems written between 1999 and 2005. The poem was based on a story I read in a local paper about a husband and father who was arrested for murder and found to be wearing women's panties. The story focused more on this fact than the actual crime, which I thought disturbing; if not predictable of American media. I later translated this poem, along with some prose poems, into French; and back into English, etc.

These are the English to French and French to English versions of the poem:

L'ART SECRET DE POESIE

Ce poème est comme l'homme qui habille dans la lingerie de sa femme. Le poème parade autour de la chambre à coucher dans son soutien-gorge noir, son slip, ses jarretelles et ses hauts talons. Le visage est un masque de cauchemar voyant : L'eye-liner bleu, long truquer des mèches, le rubis de boucle rouge à lèvres rouge, les joues fardés rouges et la perruque blonde. Ce poème est un grand secret, caché de la vue. Le poème danse autour de la pièce qui lui-même admire dans le miroir en pied. Le poème prend lui-même tombant dans l'amour avec sa propre extinction. Il chante et danse et a même des moments d'extase, comme le St. Theresa. Ce poème est au-delà de sa propre compréhension. Ce n'est pas même subtil. La femme est au travail. Les enfants sont à l'érudition d'école pour lire et écrire. Ils étudient l'art secret de poésie.

The SECRET ART OF POESIE

This poem is as the man that dresses in the lingerie of his woman.
The poem parades around the bedroom in his support throat black,
his underpants, its garters and its high heels. The face is a mask of
nightmare visionary: The blue, long eye-liner to fake wicks, the ruby
of red buckle to red lips, the red disguised cheeks and the blond wig.
This poem is a big secret, hidden view. The poem dances around the
piece that admires itself in the mirror in foot. The poem takes itself
falling in the love with his own extinction. It sings and dances and
has even moments of ecstasy, as the St. Theresa. This poem is
beyond his own comprehension. This is not even subtle. The
woman is at the work. The children are at the school erudition to
read and to write. They study the secret art of poetry.

I preferred the English to French to English version & include that in
'Man Imitating a Cloud.'

CHATEAU TIVOLI was written in 1999 in San Francisco and is
dedicated to J after we saw a performance by Marcel Marceau. I had
first seen him perform as a child. This was my third time seeing one
of the great artists of the 20th century. I am grateful for the
experience. I felt, that night in 90 minutes, watching that great poet, I
learned more about poetry than reading dozens of books and years of
study. This was the year my work began to move in a very different
direction.

SAYING THINGS. This is the only poem that survived a series I attempted after watching a heartbreaking documentary about Genie, which is a pseudonym for the *feral child* that was discovered by authorities strapped to a potty chair in California in 1970. She was thirteen years old and had suffered one of the worst cases of human isolation, neglect and abuse recorded in medical history. I was obsessed with this story and read everything I could find on her and the subject of 'language theories' and 'language disorders' because she became a test-subject for scientists, psychiatrists and especially linguists; since she didn't speak. I am still haunted by Genie's horrific story and keep a photo of her on my wall to remind me that the poem is *not* important. This poem was my private attempt to come as close to 'communicating' with her as I could get. She is now 55 years old and lives in a state facility in California.

LAST DAYS was written in memory of my grandmother Helen-Doyle Irving.

COMING INTO TOUCH was written after undergoing a complete series of *Hokomi* body centered psychotherapy sessions in 1993-1994. This modality was created by Ron Kurtz in the 1970's. I also read Norman O. Browne's 'Love's Body' for the first time, which was serendipitous.

"Freedom is poetry, taking liberties with words, breaking the rules of normal speech, violating common sense. Freedom is violence."

"The human body is not a thing or substance, given, but a continuous creation. The human body is an energy system which is never a complete structure; never static; is in perpetual inner self-construction and self-destruction; we destroy in order to make it new."

~Norman O. Brown

ASKING A BLESSING based on the painting by Nicolas Maes, 1656, which I first saw in an art book at Bard College in 1986. My first wife and I had a print of that painting in our kitchen in Rhinebeck from 1987-1990. I dreamed of seeing it in person; and had the chance during a *lost weekend* in Amsterdam in 1991. Finally, my second 'wife' J and I saw it on one of our many museum tours and she took this photo of me with the painting in 2006. This poem is dedicated to my grandparents Helen and Washington Irving and the memory of Johnny Cash. (See photo on next page)

BOOK III: THE OPENING OF THE HEART was composed in one week after seeing Bill Viola's extraordinary emotional and beautiful video installation 'Going Forth By Day' at the Guggenheim in 2002. I spent 90 minutes in the gallery and filled a notebook with notes, reflections and commentary on the impact of the work as I moved around observing the video from different angles and positions. It remains one of the most powerful and memorable 'art' experiences I have had in recent years.

www.ingramcontent.com/pod-product-compliance
Lightning Source LLC
Chambersburg PA
CBHW031828090426
42741CB00005B/169